BUFFALO SONG

BY

JOSEPH BRUCHAC

ILLUSTRATED BY

BILL FARNSWORTH

LEE & LOW BOOKS Inc.

New York

ACKNOWLEDGMENTS

My own interest in buffalo started when I was a child standing in front of a pen at the Catskill Game Farm in upstate New York, watching a small herd of the dark, powerful creatures. I was close enough to reach out my hand and almost touch one of the animals before my grandfather gently pulled me back. Even before I knew how central those great creatures were to the old ways of our American Indian nations, I felt a connection to them that has grown and deepened throughout my life.

I first began to learn the story of how the buffalo were saved from extinction when I was ten years old and read Zane Grey's nonfiction tale of Buffalo Jones, one of the men who helped preserve the American bison. In the years since then I have read many other volumes, including *The Time of the Buffalo* by Tom McHugh and *The Buffalo Book: The Full Saga of the American Animal* by David A. Dary.

Books, however, only tell part of the story. Over the years I have learned just as much through my eyes and ears, through seeing and being in close contact with herds of buffalo in many places on this continent, including the Onondaga Nation of central New York, the Cheyenne River Reservation of South Dakota, the Wichita Mountains Wildlife Refuge in Oklahoma, and the Flathead Indian Reservation on the National Bison Range near Moiese, Montana. There the buffalo themselves have taught me—just by being themselves.

Then there are the stories and songs of the buffalo that have been shared with me over the past four decades by American Indian tradition bearers and storytellers. Harold Littlebird of Laguna Pueblo, Gayle Ross of the Cherokee Nation, Swift Eagle of Santo Domingo Pueblo, and Dewasentah of the Onondaga Nation are only a few of the many to thank. *Ktsi Wliwini nitobak, wli dogo wôngan*—Great thanks, all my friends, all my relations.

A very special thanks to the Salish-Pend d'Oreille Culture Committee of the Confederated Salish and Kootenai Tribes of St. Ignatius, Montana, for putting together what I consider to be the very best book ever written about the buffalo from the perspective of Native peoples. *I Will Be Meat for My Salish People*, written by Bon I. Whealdon and others and edited by Robert Bigart, was published in 2001 by Salish Kootenai College several years after I had completed my first drafts of *Buffalo Song*. I have been working on this story for more than twelve years. Sometimes the shortest books take the longest time to complete. In this case, taking my time was a true blessing. If I had not been given a copy of *I Will Be Meat for My Salish People* while lecturing and storytelling in Montana, the book you now hold in your hands would have been quite different and much less accurate.

JOSEPH BRUCHAC

Library of Congress Cataloging-in-Publication Data • Bruchac, Joseph. Buffalo song / by Joseph Bruchac ; illustrated by Bill Farnsworth. p. cm. Summary: "The story of the first efforts to save the vanishing bison (buffalo) herds from extinction in the United States in the 1870s and 1880s. Based on the true story of Samuel Walking Coyote, a Salish (Kalispel) Indian who rescued and raised orphaned buffalo calves"—Provided by publisher. ISBN 978-1-58430-280-3 1. Walking Coyote—Juvenile literature. 2. Kalispel Indians—Biography—Juvenile literature. 3. Kalispel Indians—Social conditions—Juvenile literature. 4. American bison—Montana—Little Bitterroot River—Juvenile literature. 5. Wildlife conservation—Montana—Little Bitterroot River—Juvenile literature. I. Farnsworth, Bill, ill. II. Title. E99.K17.B78   2008   305.897'94350092—dc22   [B]   2007024912

To the memory of Michael Lacapa, artist, storyteller, writer, and friend
and
To all those, past and present, who have worked to save the Buffalo People
—J.B.

For Cait —B.F.

Long ago there were no buffalo on Earth. Sun Buffalo Cow looked down from the sky and saw that the humans were suffering.

"I will go and change into Earth Buffalo," she sang. "I will be meat for my Indian people."

Her words were heard by the humans below. Then Sun Buffalo Cow ran along the trail that led to the cliff. She leaped from that high place to the foot of the cliff far below.

The people came along then and saw the dead buffalo. "Our mother has spoken truly," they said. "Here is food for us."

Then they heard the sound of hooves rumbling like thunder. They looked out and saw great herds of buffalo covering the earth.

—FROM A TRADITIONAL SALISH STORY

It was a dark day in 1873. On the grassy floor of the canyon a buffalo calf pressed her nose against her mother's flank. The thunder sounds were gone, along with the men and their wagons. All the other animals in the small herd lay still on the earth around her. Their sheltered place in the mountains had not protected them. The hunters had taken only the tongues of the buffalo they killed.

The calf had come from the brush where she had lain hidden. Her mother was the oldest cow and the leader of the herd. She was the one who had always guided the herd away from danger. The calf nudged her mother again, but the large cow did not move. Night came and the calf huddled close to her mother's cold side.

The sun rose and set two times before a horse carrying two Nez Perce riders came into the canyon. The hooves of the Appaloosa did not clatter on the rocks, for it did not wear the iron shoes of a white man's horse. The boy looked around from behind his father, saddened but not surprised at what he saw. Just then the buffalo calf lifted her head. She was so weak from hunger she could neither stand nor run away.

The boy leaped down and ran to the calf's side, cradling her head in his lap.

"This one still lives," he said. "Can we help her, Father?"

The boy's father, Two Swans, climbed down from the horse's back and let the reins trail on the ground. He put his hand on his son's shoulder and squeezed it gently.

"Red Elk, a little one like this takes much care," he said. "We have a long way to go and this calf is too weak to travel with us."

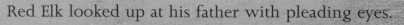

Red Elk looked up at his father with pleading eyes.

Two Swans smiled. "All right, my son. We will not leave her," he said.
"I have a friend who lives near here. He has been gathering together
such orphans to help the Buffalo People survive. His hope is that our
children's grandchildren will hear their hooves thunder across the plains
again. His name is Walking Coyote. He will be glad to see this little one."

Two Swans slid his arms under the calf and carried her to his horse.
The horse stood quietly as he placed the calf across its back and then
climbed on. Red Elk vaulted up behind his father. They rode in the
direction of the sunset toward the mountains.

The sun was in the middle of the sky when Two Swans and
Red Elk reached a camp in the shadow of the highest point in
the mountains. The scent of other buffalo reached the calf's nose.
She struggled to raise her head and look.

With the help of his son, Two Swans lowered the calf to the ground
and placed her on her wobbly legs. There, in a corral made of brush and
saplings tied together, was a handful of other buffalo calves.

A man standing by the corral's entrance raised a hand in greeting.
Behind the corral was a small shelter, where a woman and a teenage
boy were cooking their midday meal over a fire. The woman and boy
stayed where they were as the man walked forward.

"Two Swans," the man called. "It's good to see you!"

"Walking Coyote, my old friend. Good to see you too," Two Swans replied. He took Walking Coyote's hand. "My son found another orphan for you to add to your family. Hunters got her herd. She's the last."

As Walking Coyote approached, the calf lowered her head and tried to stomp her hoof in defiance. But the calf's legs were too weak and she stumbled. Only Red Elk's quick motion to grab the calf prevented her from falling.

Walking Coyote reached out his left hand to stroke the calf. As he did so, Red Elk saw a braided bracelet of buffalo tail hairs on the man's wrist.

"My young friend," Walking Coyote said. "When I was four winters old I saw my first herd of buffalo. I was riding with my uncle. We came to a hill in Sinyelemin, our Surrounded Valley on the other side of these mountains. The whole earth was black with buffalo. The herd stretched from one horizon to the other. That was almost thirty years ago. Have you ever seen anything like that?"

Red Elk shook his head no.

"It was the most beautiful thing I've ever seen," Walking Coyote said. "I've never forgotten it."

Walking Coyote slid the buffalo hair bracelet from his wrist and placed it in the boy's hand. "This is to help you remember what I saw."

There was no need for Red Elk to speak words of thanks. Walking Coyote knew what was in his heart. Red Elk walked back to his father, who reached down to pull his son up behind him on their horse. Without looking back, they rode away.

Walking Coyote lifted the calf and carried her toward the corral. She struggled weakly until he began to sing in a soft voice.

Hetcha hey
Hetcha ho
Hetcha hey yeh ho

Then Walking Coyote placed the calf gently on her feet in the corral. She leaned against him, lightly thumping her foot on the ground.

"You are a brave one, my Little Thunder Hoof," Walking Coyote said. "Your Buffalo People kept my people alive. You gave us food and shelter. Now it's my turn to help you. I'm going to take you and these others across the mountains. The Black Robe Fathers, the Catholic priests at St. Ignatius Mission, have good pastureland. They care about our souls. Surely they will care for you who make our spirits stronger."

Walking Coyote's wife brought over a bowl and placed it in front of Little Thunder Hoof.

"This is my wife, Mary," Walking Coyote told the calf. "You better thank her. This was her idea too. Mary, tell this little one what you said to me."

Mary smiled and looked at her husband. "The buffalo that our Salish people love will soon be gone. We are sad because of that. You capture what calves you can and take them to our people. When they see the buffalo, they'll be glad."

The teenage boy came and stood beside the calf.

"This is our son, Blanket Hawk," Walking Coyote said.

Blanket Hawk gently pressed the calf's nose down toward the bowl, which held a watery mixture of porridge and roots. As the scent of the food filled the calf's nostrils, she lowered her head and began to eat.

Walking Coyote watched and nodded in approval. "By the time the snow leaves the passes," he said, "you'll be ready to journey over the mountains."

The sun rose and set many times. Little Thunder Hoof grew strong and began playing with the other calves. As they butted heads and chased after one another it became clear to Walking Coyote, Mary, and Blanket Hawk that Little Thunder Hoof was taking control as the leader of their small herd. All the calves knew and trusted the three humans who were caring for them, but they did not come when they were called until Little Thunder Hoof led them.

"Little Thunder Hoof, it's a good thing you've become a leader of your people," Walking Coyote said. "We'll need your help to get all of you safely across the mountains. It's not going to be an easy journey."

By midsummer, the Moon When Buffalo Shed Their Winter Coats, more buffalo calf orphans had been brought to Walking Coyote. The little herd now numbered nine—five bull calves and four cow calves.

Early one morning Walking Coyote looked up at the high mountains and then at the small herd that had come up to the edge of the corral.

"My friends, it's a fine day for us to travel," Walking Coyote said.

Blanket Hawk came to the corral and reached out a hand to stroke the nose of Little Thunder Hoof. "I've scouted ahead," he said. "I know the way well. I've found water for you to drink, grass for you to eat, and places where you can shelter for the night."

Mary laughed. "If you two keep talking to the calves, we'll still be here at nightfall. Let's go."

Mary pulled aside the brush that blocked the corral's entrance. Led by Little Thunder Hoof, the herd came trotting out. They followed their human protectors up the slope that led to the mountain passes.

The trail was difficult. There were places where they had to wade through streams or climb over fallen trees. Sometimes Walking Coyote and Mary had to carry the smallest calves, or sling them over the back of a packhorse, when their legs grew too tired to carry them any farther.

At night when they made camp, Walking Coyote spoke to Little Thunder Hoof and the other calves.

"Be watchful, little ones," he said. "There are wolves and mountain lions here who may catch your scent." Then he sang his song to calm the calves and give them courage.

Hetcha hey
Hetcha ho
Hetcha hey yeh ho

For the first two nights all went well. But on the third day, as they neared a high pass, wolf eyes watched them from behind the small pines. The way was steep, and one of the smaller calves fell behind. The lone wolf crept closer.

Little Thunder Hoof lifted her head to sniff the wind. Catching a scent that meant danger, she turned and charged down the hill. The wolf had cornered the small calf against a rock outcropping. Little Thunder Hoof lowered her head and thudded her hoof hard on the earth. The wolf turned and ran down the mountain.

Walking Coyote and Blanket Hawk watched, smiles on their faces, as the wolf disappeared around the slope.

"Little Thunder Hoof," Blanket Hawk said, hugging the calf. "You have the heart of a leader indeed!"

Little Thunder Hoof nuzzled Blanket Hawk's face. Then she turned and butted her head against the side of the small calf, herding it back up toward the others.

More days passed and the herd began its descent down the western side of the mountains. The path was steep and rocky. As they made their way along a narrow ridge, Little Thunder Hoof turned and looked up, stomping her hoof. A distant rumbling began to grow louder. The mountain growled. The earth started to shake beneath them.

"Landslide!" Mary shouted. She waved her arms and drove the calves after Little Thunder Hoof, who was leading them toward a great rock that might provide shelter. Blanket Hawk and Walking Coyote each grabbed a small calf from the edge of the ridge. Loose earth and huge boulders cascaded past them in a waterfall of stones.

When all was calm Walking Coyote counted heads. One of the bull calves was gone, carried away by the rock slide. Had it not been for Little Thunder Hoof, several more calves could have been lost.

Walking Coyote's heart was filled with hope as he led the little
herd toward St. Ignatius Mission.

"We do not want to part with you," he told the buffalo calves.
"But my family is poor. I will give you to the Black Robe Fathers.
They will take good care of you."

But the priests at the mission did not want Walking Coyote's animals.

"I thought they would understand how the buffalo strengthen our spirit," Walking Coyote said sadly.

"Don't worry," Mary replied. "Our Salish people who live near here will be glad to see the buffalo. They will help us care for them."

Sure enough, as word of the arrival of the buffalo calves spread through the valley, people were happy. A feast was given for Walking Coyote, Mary, and Blanket Hawk.

"Our brother and his family have brought us a gift," the Salish chief said.

Life was not easy for Walking Coyote and his family. Driving the herd from pasture to pasture as the seasons changed took all their time and energy. One winter came and then another. The buffalo calves grew into adults. In the third spring after crossing into the valley, Little Thunder Hoof and the three other cows all gave birth to calves.

The buffalo roamed free, and Walking Coyote was glad to see the herd grow larger with each passing year. Walking Coyote's own family grew larger too. He and Mary had three daughters. They worked hard over the years, but still they were poor. It was now 1884.

"My buffalo children, we need help," Walking Coyote said. "If only we could find someone else who remembers how beautiful it was when the Buffalo People blanketed the plains."

Michel Pablo was such a person. His father was Mexican and his mother a Piegan Indian. He had come to the valley to work many years ago and had become a wealthy rancher. On his rides through the countryside he had often seen Walking Coyote's herd. The sight of it made him feel good in his heart.

He went to Walking Coyote with an offer.

"I like your dream of bringing back the buffalo," Michel Pablo said. "Our valley is a good place for a herd. We have wide pastures, shelter from the winter storms, and plenty of Indian people who love these animals. Let me buy your herd from you."

It was hard for Walking Coyote to part with the buffalo who had been with his family for so long. But finally he sighed and nodded.

"My friend," Walking Coyote said, "I will trust you with my children."

And so it was done. Little Thunder Hoof and the other buffalo
saved by Walking Coyote and his family passed into the care of
Michel Pablo. There in the shadow of the mountains by the Flathead
River the buffalo found a good home. Soon Michel Pablo went into
partnership with Charles Allard, another rancher who remembered
the time of the buffalo.

The Pablo-Allard herd grew into the hundreds. For many years
Walking Coyote, his family, and the Salish people looked with pride
at the herd that held their spirit. It reminded them of the time when
they and the buffalo had shared the land. As they listened to the
rumble of buffalo hooves in the valley, from somewhere between
the earth and the sky, it seemed they could hear a song:

> Hetcha hey
> Hetcha ho
> Hetcha hey yeh ho

AFTERWORD

Whista Shinchilapi, Samuel Walking Coyote, passed on in 1897, Mary in 1901. The Pablo-Allard herd continued to grow and thrive on the Flathead Indian Reservation. Then the United States government announced that in 1907 the reservation would be opened to white settlers and the valley broken up into small allotments of land. The free range needed for the buffalo to graze would no longer exist. Pablo and Allard offered to sell their herd to the government, but Congress failed to approve the deal. Finally the Canadian government agreed to purchase the herd. The roundup began in 1906, but it was difficult getting the buffalo loaded onto railroad freight cars. In 1909 the last animals that could be caught were put on a train. Those that were not captured were left behind on the Flathead Reservation. In all, about seven hundred buffalo were shipped 1,200 miles to Buffalo National Park in Alberta, Canada.

Walking Coyote is not the only one credited with helping to save the buffalo from extinction. Several farsighted groups and individuals in the late nineteenth century and early twentieth century worked to preserve the wild buffalo. These included the Smithsonian Institution, the New York Zoological Society, and the American Bison Society. President Theodore Roosevelt set aside land for three reserves for the preservation of the buffalo, which led to the establishment of the National Bison Range in Montana in 1908. The United States government then bought back from Canada some of the Pablo-Allard herd to live on the National Bison Range.

Today the buffalo are no longer endangered. Descendants of Walking Coyote's orphans and the Pablo-Allard herd can be found in many protected natural areas in the United States. In addition to the National Bison Range, these include Yellowstone National Park in Wyoming, Wichita Mountains Wildlife Refuge in Oklahoma, Sullys Hill National Game Preserve in North Dakota, and Neal Smith National Wildlife Refuge in Iowa. In fact, thanks to Walking Coyote and all the others who labored to save the buffalo, there are now free-roaming and ranched herds of varying sizes in almost every state and on many American Indian reservations. The commercial bison industry started in the late 1950s and began to grow rapidly in the 1980s, when demand increased for buffalo meat as a tasty and healthy alternative to beef.

Current estimates place the size of the total United States herd at about 250,000 animals. Although the great herds of yesterday will never again roam across North America, the buffalo are now abundant enough to ensure the continued well-being of this important spiritual and cultural American symbol for generations to come.

Buffalo is the commonly-used term for North American bison.